Rediscovering the Eternal Song
A Parent's Guide to Growing Musical Connection

By Gillian Corke

Bath, 2025

Dedication

For those who lost the music and are finding it again.

For those who were told they weren't musical — and the children who showed them otherwise.

For my husband and children who live this daily.

Table of Contents

Rediscovering the Eternal Song
A Parent's Guide to Growing Musical Connection 1
    Table of Contents 3
    Acknowledgements 5
Welcome Note 6
Introduction 6

        Part One: Remembering What Was Always There 8

Chapter 1 - Every Child is Musical 8
Chapter 2 - How Musicality Develops 11
Chapter 3 - Lullabies and the Sound of Safety 14
Chapter 4 - Movement Before Melody 17

       ~ Interlude ~ - Music and the Human Tendencies 20

        Part Two: Daily Life in Musical Relationship 24

Chapter 5 - Listening Before Speaking 24
Chapter 6 - The Movement of Music 28
Chapter 7 - Songs That Hold Us 31
Chapter 8 - Listening Beyond Words 34
Chapter 9 - It's Not Just for Babies 38
Chapter 10 - When Music Becomes Misunderstood 40

       ~ Interlude ~ In Practice: A Role Play of Recognition 44

        Part Three: Holding the Bigger Picture 45

Chapter 11 - When the Song is Silenced 45
Chapter 12 - When Words Aren't There 48
Chapter 13 - Sacred Sound, Silent Song 51
Chapter 14 - Rediscovering the Eternal Song 55

Glossary of Gentle Definitions...**58**
    Continue Exploring..59
    Discography & Listening List...59
        Songs from the Text.. 59
        Suggested Listening Selections.. 60
    Listening and Activity Suggestions...61
References and Further Reading..**62**
    Stay Connected..64
About the Author..**64**
    Also by the Author..65

Acknowledgements

To my neighbours, who played music to me as a baby and planted those early seeds of sound and comfort — thank you. To my parents, who supported my musical life and listened to hours (and hours) of practice with patience and encouragement.

To my teachers and fellow musicians, who offered not just instruction, but presence, friendship and play. To my sister, who inspired me daily and held her line with integrity and power. To Pandora's Band — together we learned what shared music really means. To Profoundly Deep - Your community, mentorship and friendship gave me space to grow.

To the families, children, and communities who reminded me daily of music's quiet power. To the mentors and thinkers whose work echoes throughout these pages. And to all the workshop participants who brought your stories with such honesty and heart — your courage shaped this book more than you know.

Introduction

The Music We Already Carry

This book was born from a simple question I've asked again and again: *When did the music die?*

Often, the answers come in stories.
 A child sings joyfully — then stops after one offhand remark.
 A teacher corrects pitch, and a voice withdraws.
 A parent grows up in silence and doesn't know where to begin.

We live in a world where musicality is too often commodified, corrected, or ignored. But the truth is: **every child is musical.** Every parent can be too.

This book is not a how-to guide.
 It's not a performance manual or a promise of perfect outcomes.
 It's an invitation — to return to something that is already inside you.

You might have forgotten how. You might feel awkward or uncertain. You might even be thinking, *"But I'm not musical."* That's alright. You're not alone.

Here, we'll explore how musicality lives in movement, voice, rhythm and relationship. We'll look at the science behind connection, the wisdom of traditional practices, and the everyday magic of song between child and caregiver.

You may find yourself surprised by the simplicity of some suggestions.
 Please don't mistake that for superficiality.
 A humming voice. A tapping foot. A shared laugh in rhythm.
 These are not small things — they are deeply human, and profoundly powerful.

Even now, the music hasn't disappeared. It might be quiet, hidden, waiting.

But it's there. **Come in. Join us. Listen.**

laughed. "There were verses, choruses, and a finale. No one taught him that — he just did it."

That little boy wasn't being trained — he was being musical. No adult correction, no instruction. Just expression, delight, and story — all wrapped in song.

One participant reflected, "I used to think singing with my daughter had to have a purpose — like teaching counting or spelling. But when I just let myself join her silly songs, we both smiled more."

This is where musicality lives: not in outcomes, but in presence.

A Note on Confidence

Many parents carry old stories about their own musical abilities. You may have been told to mouth the words in choir, or been laughed at for singing off-key. These messages stay with us. They shape our willingness to join in.

But here's the truth: children do not need perfect singing. They need *real singing*. They need your voice, your attention, your rhythm — not anyone else's.

A participant once said, "I was always afraid to sing in front of my kids. But then one day I just did it. My daughter said, 'Sing it again!' That was it. I never looked back."

Your child isn't waiting for a polished performance. They're waiting for you.

What to Watch For

Musicality appears early and often, especially when adults are attuned:

- The bounce and sway to a rhythm
- The babbled phrases that rise and fall in pitch
- The spoon tapping, foot stomping, toy jingling
- The made-up melodies in the bath or on a walk

These are not just cute moments. They are glimpses of a fundamental human gift.

Our role is to notice, respond, and protect that gift.

Reflection Questions

- What musical behaviours did you notice in yourself as a child?
- What stories have you inherited about being "musical" or "not musical"?
- What happens when you see your child singing or making a sound?

No need to wait. You can hum now. You can tap your fingers now. You can begin again now.

Chapter 2

How Musicality Develops

> *"Babies are in rhythm long before they are in language."*

Musicality does not arrive all at once. It grows in stages — through play, movement, repetition, and imitation — and is shaped by the relationships and environments that surround a child. It is not separate from development; it *is* development.

From the very start, babies are immersed in rhythm and sound. In the womb, they hear the mother's voice filtered through fluid and heartbeat. After birth, they begin to coo and babble, mimicking the tones they hear. These are musical utterances — explorations of pitch, rhythm, and phrasing.

When parents sing to their babies, the infant's brain responds with synchronised neural firing. Studies using EEG and MRI show that musical interaction stimulates areas involved in language, emotion, motor coordination, and even empathy. Music is not a luxury; it is a central part of the way human beings grow and bond.

> *"I remembered a song, when I was five or six. It literally had my name in it.*
>
> *My dad sang it to me a lot. My mum too. And it became part of who I was. Everyone who saw me would start singing that song."*

In the words of Dr. Laurel Trainor, a developmental psychologist and neuroscientist, "When a caregiver and baby engage in musical play, they're actually building the brain's ability to regulate emotion, anticipate patterns, and feel safe in relationship."

A Story of Discovery

Maria, a mother of two, described noticing how her son began to hum while building with blocks.

> "He'd repeat the same little tune every time," she said. "At first I thought he was just copying something from TV, but it turned out to be his own — he'd change it when the tower got taller."

That repetitive humming was not just background noise. It was regulation, storytelling, and experimentation — all wrapped in sound.

The Role of Movement

Dalcroze Eurhythmics emphasises the body as the first musical instrument. Through bouncing, swaying, and stomping, children feel rhythm in their muscles and joints. Montessori similarly recognised the importance of purposeful movement, encouraging children to internalise order and pattern through motion.

We might see this in the toddler who dances without prompting, or the child who taps out rhythms on the table. These actions are not separate from musicality — they *are* musicality.

In the workshop, one participant remembered her daughter singing nonsense syllables while twirling in the living room.

> "She was completely in her own world," she said. "I almost interrupted to ask what she was singing — then I realised, I didn't need to know."

This is a key idea: children do not always make music *for* us. Sometimes, they do it *for themselves* — and we are simply privileged to witness it.

Imitation and Belonging

Children learn by copying. Kodály's approach centres the voice — beginning with folk songs, call and response, and simple pentatonic tunes that match the child's vocal range. These early experiences allow children to *join* the musical culture around them.

But imitation is not just about learning accuracy. It's about joining a shared rhythm, contributing a voice, and feeling a sense of belonging.

One parent in a workshop session shared:

> "When I finally sang with my son, he didn't correct me. He just beamed. I realised — I was *joining his song*, not the other way around."

A Reminder

Musical development is not linear. It does not follow a fixed path. Some children sing before they speak. Others dance before they hum. Some appear quiet for years, then suddenly create rich, melodic stories.

What matters most is not *when* the musicality appears — but whether the child feels safe, seen, and supported when it does.

Reflection Questions

- What small musical behaviours have you noticed in your child?
- How do you respond when your child makes spontaneous sounds or movement?
- Were you encouraged to explore music freely as a child? What messages did you receive?

Chapter 3

Lullabies and the Sound of Safety

> *"I remember singing in the dark because I was scared. It helped me feel less alone."*

There's a quiet kind of power in a lullaby. In those soft, repeating melodies we find something ancient — a way of holding, soothing, and being with a child that goes beyond words. Across cultures and generations, lullabies have whispered the same message: *You are safe. You are loved. You can rest now.*

Long before formal music lessons or structured play, there is this — the quiet singing of a caregiver, rocking a child in rhythm. Research shows that lullabies help regulate an infant's heart rate and breathing. They increase oxytocin, the bonding hormone. They reduce cortisol, the stress hormone. They are a biological act of connection.

One parent from the workshop remembered a turning point during her daughter's colicky weeks:

> "I'd tried everything — feeding, rocking, bouncing. I was at my end and choking back tears myself. Then I started singing a lullaby my mother used to sing through the tightness in my throat. It wasn't magic, but it gave me something to do, something to hang on to, and eventually, she settled. I think I did too."

In that moment, the lullaby didn't just soothe the child — it soothed the adult. This is one of the most overlooked functions of lullabies: they co-regulate. They help everyone breathe more easily.

The Science of Soothing

Studies in developmental psychology and neuroscience highlight the significance of what's called *infant-directed singing*. This form of singing

— often slower, higher in pitch, and with exaggerated contours — is universal. Even parents who don't consider themselves musical do it instinctively.

In fact, one study (Trehub et al., 1997) found that babies remained calm twice as long when listening to singing compared to spoken words. Another study showed that live singing was more effective in reducing infant distress than recorded music (Corbeil et al., 2013).

These findings suggest something profound: it's not just the song. It's *you* — your presence, your voice, your intention.

Songs That Carry Memory

Lullabies are often one of the first places where culture and tradition are passed down musically. They carry the cadence of a language, the values of a people, the melodies of ancestors. Even made-up lullabies become family heirlooms.

One participant said, "I found myself singing a tune I didn't know I knew — later my aunt told me my grandma used to sing it to us."

Another said, "We never had lullabies in my family, so I made one up. Now my daughter sings it to her doll. That's her song now."

Whether inherited or invented, these songs form part of a child's inner world. They become the sound of safety — internalised music that can be recalled in later moments of distress or tiredness.

Singing Through Tiredness

Sometimes the hardest thing is to sing when you are exhausted, frayed, or feeling alone. But it is in those moments that lullabies matter most. Not because they fix anything, but because they hold the moment.

One mother from the session shared this:

> "There were nights when I was so tired I couldn't think of a single word. So I just hummed. That hum became *our* lullaby. It said everything I couldn't."

You don't need perfect lyrics or a great melody. You don't even need to sing out loud. A hum, a rhythm, a breath — these are lullabies too.

Reflection Questions

- Were you sung to as a child? Can you remember any of those songs?
- What happens in your body when you hum or sing softly?
- What lullaby might you carry forward — from your own childhood or one you create today?

Whether sung in full voice or whispered in the dark, lullabies are a gift. For the child, yes — but also for the parent.

They remind us that music doesn't begin with instruction. It begins with connection.

It begins with you.

Chapter 4

Movement Before Melody

"We moved and sang and touched. That's how I knew I was okay."

If music is sound in time, then movement is music in space. Before a child can sing a scale or clap in rhythm, they rock, sway, bounce, crawl. These early movements are not separate from musical development — they are its foundation.

Long before we learn to speak or sing, we feel rhythm in our bodies. In fact, we're born into it — cradled by the steady pulse of the heartbeat, lulled by the rhythms of walking, speech, and breath. This inner metronome becomes the scaffolding for musicality.

In Dalcroze Eurhythmics and Montessori practices, movement is not an add-on to music learning; it *is* music learning. The body is the first instrument. When children skip, march, spin, or sway in response to sound, they are forming essential neural connections — integrating timing, balance, coordination, and emotional expression.

The Science of Motion

Studies in motor development and early childhood education reveal strong links between physical movement and auditory processing. Movement supports rhythm perception, attention, and executive functioning. Dancing to a beat is not just a fun activity — it's training the brain to predict, synchronise, and adapt.

One study (Williams et al., 2015) found that rhythmic movement activities in preschool were directly related to improvements in self-regulation and social cooperation. These aren't just nice side effects — they're vital outcomes for school readiness and lifelong wellbeing.

A Moment at Home

A father from the workshop recalled a morning routine:

> "My daughter would make me 'march' with her down the hall every day before breakfast. We had this silly beat we'd stomp to. It was fun. It always made us laugh, and I realised — this was music. This was learning."

These moments are more than play. They're bonding, pattern recognition, and body awareness — wrapped in joy.

Modeling, Not Managing

It can be tempting to gamify or commoditise these movements — to add points, prizes, or tasks. But movement for its own sake is already valuable. The role of the adult is to model — to *show* rather than *instruct*.

Jump. Twist. Pause. Flow. Vary your movements and see what your child does in response. Follow their lead. Offer surprises. Let your shared motion become a conversation.

When movement is free, varied, and joyful, the child learns to inhabit rhythm, not perform it. This builds musical confidence from the inside out.

Rhythm Lives in the Body

One father shared:

> "I noticed my son rocking in the high chair when I stirred his porridge. At first, I thought it was just a wiggle. But then I realised — he was watching and matching the rhythm of my spoon with his body."

Children sense patterns everywhere. They echo it in their gestures, in the sway of their bodies, in the drumming of fingers. Movement is not separate from thought. It *is* thought in motion.

In trauma-informed practice, we recognise that children who have experienced stress or disconnection may struggle with imposed rhythm and regulation. But safe, predictable movement — especially with a loving adult — helps restore that sense of internal order. The key is to be sensitive to the child you have in front of you - not the one you think other people expect you to have.

Movement can become a re-entry into safety, expression, and trust.

Reflection Questions

- What rhythms were part of your childhood? Games, routines, rituals?
- When do you notice your child moving rhythmically or expressively?
- How might you join your child's movement today — even for a minute?

Your body is an invitation. No props needed. Just space, presence, and willingness.

~ Interlude ~

Music and the Human Tendencies

A Montessori-Inspired Reflection

> *"I thought I had to teach music. Then I realised my son was already singing to the trees. I just had to listen."*

Maria Montessori described a set of natural drives common to all humans — urges that guide development across cultures, ages and eras. These human tendencies are not academic concepts. They are living currents in your child, and in you. Music, when offered freely and playfully, nourishes them all.

Let's explore how.

Orientation

Humans have a deep need to know where they are in space, time, and relationship. Music helps us orient. A familiar song cues bedtime. A rhythm grounds a child during a transition. Sound tells us, "You are here. This is now."

Order

Children seek patterns and predictability. Music gives order without rigidity. Lullabies repeat. Nursery rhymes have verses and refrains. Clapping games are structured and satisfying. Musical order calms the nervous system. It provides safe predictability, especially in a world that can feel chaotic.

Exploration

Children are natural explorers. They bang, blow, pluck and hum. Sound is a sensory adventure. What happens when I shake this? When I sing into a bowl? What does Mum do when I tap the table like this?

One of my favourite things to do is get a variety of instruments and put them out for the children to simply explore with respect and without fear.

Music invites curiosity — not for performance, but for discovery.

Communication

Long before speech, babies communicate through tone, pitch, and rhythm. A rising "mmm?" or a playful "da-da-da!" is music. Singing with or without words, singing with your eyes, your child builds their expressive range. It lays foundations for language — and also for empathy, connection, and humour.

Social Connection

Humans are driven to belong. To join in. Music — especially in its earliest forms — is social glue. Singing together regulates, syncs, and unites. It teaches taking turns. It invites eye contact, movement, and mutual delight.

Imagination

When a child sings to a doll or taps a spoon like a drum, they are building inner worlds. Music fuels symbolic play. It connects body, image, and voice — the building blocks of creativity.

Spirituality and Wonder

Even toddlers experience awe. A hush during a song. A hum in the dark. A dance in the rain. Music helps children express reverence, longing, joy and grief — without needing adult words.

Work (Purposeful Activity)

Montessori speaks of "work" as any focused, meaningful activity. Music — when free from performance pressure — becomes this kind of work.

Singing, tapping, and listening are forms of purposeful doing. They strengthen the will and deepen concentration.

Repetition

Children repeat what feeds them. A favourite song. A silly rhyme. A clapping game. Repetition in music is not mindless — it's how the brain and body integrate rhythm, pitch and sequence.

Abstraction

As children grow, they begin to abstract from concrete experiences. A song heard once becomes internal. They can imagine it. Hum it. Transform it. Music lives inside them. And this becomes part of their thinking, memory, and creative life.

Closing Invitation

If you've ever wondered whether music is "extra" or "optional," this is your answer: music speaks to every part of the developing human. It belongs in the home as much as in the classroom — not as a curriculum, but as a connection.

Try This

Observe your child for one day. Notice where music or rhythm naturally appears — a spontaneous hum, a game with sound, a repeated song.

See if you can follow their lead instead of initiating.

What do you learn about their needs?

In Practice

During tidy-up time, instead of saying, "Clean up now," try singing a soft, repetitive phrase:

> "Away go the blocks, away, away…"

Chapter 6

The Movement of Music

"Your heartbeat was the first rhythm your child knew."

Long before words, before clapping games or circle songs, there is the heartbeat. The steady pulse a baby hears in the womb is their first rhythm — a rhythm that reflects not only the physical world but also the emotional state of the pregnant parent. When a mother feels calm, the rhythm may feel soothing. When she is stressed or fearful, the baby's experience of movement and heartbeat can reflect that too. The rise and fall of a walking parent, the gentle sway during rest — or the rapid shift of urgency — become a child's earliest experiences of movement and music.

Musicality begins here: in the safety of bodies moving in time with one another.

Rhythm in the Body

Babies don't need to be taught to move to music. They are born to do it. Neuroscientific research confirms that infants as young as two days old can detect rhythmic patterns. A 2016 study by Trainor et al. showed that infants bounced to a regular beat were more likely to synchronise socially — a reminder that rhythm is not just a musical skill but a relational one.

In Dalcroze and Montessori traditions, movement is more than a response to sound. It is the child's language of timing, phrasing, and joy. A child spinning in the kitchen, rocking on a swing, or tapping their foot against a chair leg — all are responding musically with their bodies, even if there is no sound.

> "I watched a toddler sway with the washing machine and hum a little tune to herself. There was no performance. Just presence."

By slowing down, simplifying soundscapes, and tuning into your child's responses, you are helping build the conditions for listening to flourish.

Reflection Questions

- When do you feel most listened to? What does that feel like in your body?
- When does your child listen deeply? What are they responding to?
- How might you create small moments of quiet noticing together today?
- What thoughts, feelings or decisions come up for you when you try to listen from stillness?

In a noisy world, listening is a radical act. It says: I hear you. You matter. And in the space between sound and silence, music begins to grow.

This brings order and flow — without coercion. Your child may resist less because it feels like shared activity, not demand.

Part Two: Daily Life in Musical Relationship

Chapter 5

Listening Before Speaking

"Children don't need performance. They need permission."

Before children make music, they listen. Before they sing, they absorb. Listening is not passive; it is the foundation of all musical and relational learning. In the early years, listening is the gateway to understanding tone, rhythm, language, and meaning. It's how babies learn what matters.

Infants are wired for sound. Within hours of birth, they prefer their mother's voice to others. They recognise the melody of the language they heard in utero. And they attend differently to voices that are emotionally expressive — especially when sung.

The Art of Attuned Listening

In music education, listening is often treated as an advanced skill — something to be introduced once a child can identify instruments or follow a melody. But listening starts much earlier, and its roots are relational.

When you pause and truly listen to your child — not to correct, or judge, or plan your response, but to *receive* — you model something powerful. You show that sound carries meaning. That voice deserves space. That silence is not empty.

One parent shared:

> "My son would hum while building blocks, and I used to ignore it. One day, I stopped and listened. He was repeating a pattern over

and over. I copied it back, and his face just lit up. It was like we had a secret language."

This moment wasn't instructional. It was relational. Musical connection begins with this kind of shared attention.

What to Listen For

- Does your child hum when playing?
- Do they mimic sirens, birdsong, the rhythm of a train?
- Do they make up sound effects or play with pitch and tone?

These are all signs of an active musical brain. Listening isn't just about music — it's about the world.

A teacher trained in the Kodály approach once said:

> "When I train young ears, I don't start with music. I start with noticing: how does your mother's voice sound when she's tired? What does the wind sound like through leaves? Can you hear your own footsteps change on the stairs?"

This kind of listening builds presence. It trains attention. And it supports emotional regulation, empathy, and language development.

Creating Listening Environments

Before we dive in, a small note: it can be tempting to turn listening into a kind of game or achievement — especially when we're trying to support learning. Many of us were taught to treat attention like a task: something to be rewarded, managed, or measured. But here's a gentle invitation — what if listening didn't have to be 'good' or 'impressive'? What if it could simply be *shared*?

When we take the pressure off, we create room for real noticing. Noticing sound. Noticing each other. Noticing ourselves.

You don't need silence to listen. You need *space*.

- Turn off background music sometimes, and just sit.

- Let the sounds of the day come through — birds, wind, kitchen noises.
- Try whispering a phrase and inviting your child to copy it.
- Lie on the floor and listen together. What do you hear?

Children don't need constant stimulation. They need a relationship with sound.

> "There was an Irish band with a female singer, and the way she sang had such emotion. There was a little anger, frustration… I guess being a teenager it spoke to me. I remember dancing to it, but also her music was topical — it was about the political situation in Ireland where I lived.
>
> A thing I didn't realise at the time — we have a style of music in Ireland which is sorrowful, mourning music, like when you're grieving. This singer used that ancient style of singing. Sinéad O'Connor did that too.
>
> The band was The Cranberries. The song is 'Zombie.' It's upset, it's sad, and it helps me now too… when I'm upset or sad about the world, it helps me shake some of that out."

Listening and Trauma

For some children, especially those who have experienced adversity, listening can be difficult. Noise may feel overwhelming. Certain tones or patterns may trigger stress responses. It is important to work with others in the environment or seek expert outside assistance if you have any concerns in this area. Blanket use of ear defenders is, sadly, a short term solution to an often solvable long-term problem with the right guidance.

Neuroscience research shows that the auditory system is closely linked to the autonomic nervous system. When children feel safe, they can process sound more clearly. When stressed, their brain may shift into hyper- or hypo-sensitivity, making listening hard.

These small, everyday actions are full of meaning. They are the early architecture of rhythm, and they need space to grow.

Modelling Without Demanding

One of the most helpful things we can do is show, not tell. Children learn through mirroring — not through instruction. A parent swaying gently to music while cooking, or walking with a rhythmic step during school drop-off, is offering a kind of invitation. No praise needed, no goal set.

- Try rocking together on the sofa in time with a lullaby.
- Stomp your feet while reading a story with strong rhythm.
- Tap two spoons together as you wait for the toast.
- You could be brave and test out some sounds on the equipment at the playground or in the woods

These movements need not be 'good' or 'correct.' They simply need to be *shared*.

One parent shared:

> "I used to feel silly dancing around the house. But once I stopped caring and just joined in, my child started copying me — not because I asked, just because I was there."

A Gentle Word About Gamifying

It's so natural to want to make musical movement fun — to turn it into a game, to reward effort, or encourage a 'right way' to move. But when we tie movement to outcomes, we risk turning an expressive act into a performance.

Instead of saying, "Good dancing! You get a star!", we might simply share in the moment: "That looked like fun," or even just join in ourselves.

Children don't need applause. They need company.

Movement and Safety

For some children, especially those with a history of trauma, certain movements can feel unsafe. How this expresses itself and what triggers it varies greatly from person to person and it is essential that you are in tune with the child in front of you and not one you have read about or someone else's child. Again, seeking assistance from an expert such as Developmental Trauma specialists can be transformative.

Bodies may carry sensorial memories of chaos or stillness that didn't soothe. The nervous system — especially the brainstem — is deeply influenced by rhythm. Predictable, loving movement helps the body find its beat again.

Rocking, bouncing, walking in step — these aren't just musical experiences. They are ways of restoring regulation. Trauma-informed approaches recognise that co-regulation often begins with motion before words. By offering your presence and a steady rhythm, you're offering something deeper than instruction. You're offering trust.

Reflection Questions

- What kinds of movement made you feel safe or joyful as a child, if any?
- Where in your daily life could rhythm return — walking, chores, rest?
- How do you feel when you move musically with your child?
- Are there any movements or patterns that are a "no-go" for you? Be curious about these and journal what you notice.

Music lives in the body. And every shared step, every sway or bounce, is a line in the song we're writing together.

Let's keep moving, gently — in rhythm, and in relationship.

Chapter 7

Songs That Hold Us

> *"Music was a way to survive, to belong — even when our native songs had to be hidden."*

Wherever there are people, there are songs. Songs to welcome, songs to mourn, songs to work, songs to teach. Across time and culture, song has carried meaning where words alone could not. And for young children, traditional songs carry the pulse of heritage, connection, and care.

These songs are not always polished. Some are simple, repetitive, or even odd by modern standards. But each one is rooted in relationship — passed from mouth to ear, from lap to lap, across generations.

Songs Across Cultures

Let's look at three traditional songs from different parts of the world. Each one holds a different purpose — and a glimpse into how music lives in daily life.

Hungary – Lullaby *"Tente baba, tente"* is a soft Hungarian lullaby. Its simple melody and rocking rhythm have soothed children for centuries. The words are minimal — a gentle instruction to sleep — but the melody carries the emotional weight.

This song has been used in countless Hungarian households as a nightly ritual, helping babies transition into rest while also offering calm to the adult singing it. The predictability of the song — same tune, same rocking — gives the nervous system a cue: you are safe now.

South Africa – Play Song From Zulu traditions comes *"Thula Thula,"* a song often sung in play or gently while a child is carried. The refrain —

"hush, hush" — is soothing but also rhythmic. It allows for movement, clapping, and interaction.

This kind of song lives in the shared space between adult and child, inviting musical communication. It is both bonding and playful — often accompanied by dancing or mimicry.

Japan – Seasonal Song *"Sakura Sakura"* is a Japanese folk melody tied to the cherry blossom season. Though often sung by older children and adults, it connects even young listeners to the rhythm of the natural world and the emotional cycle of the year — blooming, fading, returning.

A parent singing this while walking under blossoms with their child is not just marking the season. They are linking memory, beauty, and cultural identity through music.

Inviting the Songs In

Traditional songs offer a ready-made path into shared musical life. If you've ever felt unsure about singing with your child, these songs offer a gentle entry point. There's no need to perform or impress. These songs were never meant for concert halls — they were meant for kitchens, fields, laps, and arms.

They don't require special training or perfect pitch. They just need a voice, a listener, and a little time.

One parent shared:

> "I started singing an old lullaby my grandmother used to sing to me. At first it felt strange — I hadn't sung in years. But my daughter nestled in, and now it's ours."

The songs we bring from our own childhood — or choose to learn now — offer a kind of belonging. You don't need to sing in your ancestral language to share in this. Choose a song that feels right. Learn it slowly. Let it grow in your voice.

More Than a Melody

Research shows that traditional lullabies and play songs help regulate infants' heart rates, calm stress responses, and support language development (Trehub & Trainor, 1998). But their deeper value lies in connection. These songs are often delivered in close proximity, with eye contact, rhythm, and attunement. They are musical co-regulation.

For children who have experienced early disruption or inconsistent care, these songs can become anchoring. For parents unsure of how to connect through words, song can be a bridge.

Reflection Questions

- Are there any songs from your childhood you remember hearing or singing?
- What song might you bring into your family rhythm — at bedtime, bath time, or in play?
- Can you try singing a simple traditional song this week — without needing it to be perfect?

Your voice, offered with warmth and repetition, is more powerful than any playlist.

These songs are not entertainment. They are nourishing. And they are waiting to be sung.

Chapter 8

Listening Beyond Words

"I stopped trying to fill the space with instructions… and she told me more through her humming than she ever did with words."

Music is not only sound. It is listening — deep, responsive, attuned listening. Before children sing or play, they listen. And long after a song ends, the listening continues. Listening is how we feel each other's rhythms, moods, pauses. It is how we begin to belong.

Children are listening all the time — not just to what we say, but how we say it, what we hum, how we pause. In musical terms, they are always attuning. Our tone, our pacing, our silence — all these become part of their inner song.

Listening as Connection

Developmentally, listening is the foundation of communication. From the final trimester in utero, babies begin responding to voice and melody. Studies (Partanen et al., 2013) show that newborns recognise lullabies they heard in the womb, responding with lowered heart rates and calm attention. Even without language, listening creates a sense of familiarity and safety.

Attuned listening fosters connection. It is a cornerstone of interpersonal neurobiology (Siegel, 2012). When a caregiver listens with presence — really listens — the child's brain begins to map the world as safe, responsive, and co-regulated. This is not just emotional support. It is biological scaffolding for empathy and relational skills.

> "When I stopped trying to fill the space with instructions, and just listened — really listened — my daughter told me more through her songs than she ever did with words."

When the Music Goes Quiet

Sometimes, children stop singing. A child who once sang constantly now hums only when alone. Another stops initiating musical play, or grows shy at the sound of their own voice. These quiet moments can be easily overlooked — but they are often full of meaning.

Withdrawal from musical expression can signal disconnection, fear of judgment, or a need for more safety. In trauma-informed terms, this may reflect a shift into a protective state: the child has assessed, however unconsciously, that their musical voice is not welcome.

One participant in our workshop reflected:

> "I used to sing all the time. But after a while, I realised it only annoyed the grown-ups around me. I learned to sing inside my head."

When children go quiet, it doesn't mean the music has vanished. It may be waiting — quietly, carefully — for safety to return.

The Power of Being Heard

In one of the workshop sessions, a participant shared how being constantly silenced in childhood — told to stop singing, to stop making noise — affected her confidence as a parent.

> "My daughter would sing and I'd want to say 'not now.' But I heard my own little voice in her. I realised I needed to learn to listen to her the way I wish someone had listened to me."

This is not uncommon. Many of us carry early memories of being unheard — of being told we were too loud, too messy, off-key, or just annoying. Listening with openness now can begin to rewrite that story, for us and for our children.

Active Listening in Practice

Listening doesn't mean silence. It means presence. We listen with our eyes, our posture, our attention. We listen by slowing down, pausing before responding, or letting the moment linger.

Here are a few gentle ways to practise musical listening with your child:

- Hum back the tune your child is singing without correcting or leading it.
- Pause when they stop singing — let them choose the next moment.
- Echo back a rhythm they tapped with your own body — a clap, a tap, a sway.
- Let silence sit after music. Don't rush to talk.

This kind of listening isn't only musical. It is relational. It tells the child: "You matter. I'm here. I hear you."

When Listening Is Hard

Some parents find this harder than expected. For those who grew up in noisy or unsafe environments, silence can feel threatening. For others, the impulse to teach or fix is strong.

That's okay. You can start small. One minute of shared stillness. One moment of just noticing your child's humming without response. The goal isn't perfection — it's presence.

> "I learned that my son sang most when he thought no one was listening. So I let him have that. I listened without interrupting. Now, he sings to me."

Reflection Questions

- What kind of listening did you grow up with?
- How does it feel to simply listen to your child's voice, without responding?

- Can you find one moment today to practise attuned listening — musically or otherwise?

When we learn to listen beyond words, we rediscover a deeper language — one that holds, reflects, and invites.

And in that quiet presence, something ancient sings back to us.

Chapter 9

It's Not Just for Babies

How Musical Connection Grows With Your Child

"He's seven now, but he still melts when I hum the lullaby I used to sing when he was tiny."

There's a common idea that musical connection — the lullabies, the gentle rhythms, the cooing and rocking — belongs only in babyhood. And while it's true that music is vital in those earliest months, it doesn't stop being meaningful once a child can walk or talk.

In fact, the opposite is true.

The nervous system we soothe in infancy doesn't disappear — it matures. The child's need for rhythm, resonance, and connection doesn't fade — it evolves.

Older children still benefit from co-regulation, from tone, from tempo, from the embodied presence that music brings. But they may receive it differently. Not as a lullaby, but as a shared playlist. Not as rocking, but as drumming. Not as humming in arms, but as dancing side by side in the kitchen.

One parent shared that her child, now eight, insists she stop singing out loud — "It's embarrassing!" — yet quietly sits on the sofa when she plays the ukulele and sings softly to herself. A connection remains. It's just quieter now, more oblique. But it's there.

A teacher described how her Year 6 students settle more easily when she plays a gentle instrumental piece at the start of each lesson. She never introduces it, never comments — it's simply a signal: "We're here. We're arriving. Let's begin." The children begin to sync to the pace of the music without instruction.

Another parent recalled how her teenage son, who no longer tolerates hugs, sang the family lullaby back to her under his breath when she was unwell. No explanation. Just a moment of shared understanding, held in melody.

These are the same patterns we laid down in infancy — rhythmic, relational, regulating. They grow with the child. They are not outgrown.

Music still makes space for feelings that don't yet have words. For children navigating school stress, social shifts, identity, anger, loss — music can hold and transform what might otherwise get buried.

The key, as always, is presence. Not performance. Listening together. Being alongside. Noticing.

Reflection Questions

- What moments of musical connection are already alive between you and your child, even if unspoken?
- Are there rhythms or rituals from their babyhood that might gently return — in a new form?
- How does your older child respond when music is simply there, not directed at them, but present?

Chapter 10

When Music Becomes Misunderstood

> *"I used to sing until they told me to stop. Then I learned to sing inside my head."*

Not all musical behaviour is welcomed. Some parents tell me their child sings too much, too loudly, or too strangely. Others describe resistance: a child who won't join in, who hides when the music starts, who acts out when songs are sung.

This is where our understanding of child behaviour — and misbehaviour — meets the world of music.

The Mistaken Goals in Music

Rooted in Adlerian psychology, the "Mistaken Goals" framework suggests that children's challenging behaviours are driven by unmet needs for belonging and significance. They may not yet have the skills or words to express what they need, so they use behaviour to try to get their needs met — even if the results are counterproductive. Personally, I like to call them "Mistaken Strategies" - the goal is legitimate. We all want to belong, be able to contribute and be protected. The strategy - how we can unconsciously choose to get this "because it works" - is the mistaken part. But even then, to the young mind, there's no mistake. The strategy works.

How about we put a different lens on it and respond to what the child is asking for - connection, rather than react to the way they ask?

Here's how this might show up in music:

- **Undue Attention**: A child insists on being the centre of the song, interrupts others' music-making, or demands praise for every note. The adult feels irritated. Underneath may be a fear of not being seen or valued.
- **Power**: A child refuses to join in, mocks the activity, or takes control of the instrument and won't share. The adult feels challenged. This may signal a need for autonomy or influence, especially if they often feel powerless.
- **Revenge**: A child disrupts songs, makes hurtful parodies, or criticises others. The adult feels hurt or disgusted. This can be a response to emotional wounds, where the child feels hurt and wants others to feel it too.
- **Assumed Inadequacy**: A child says, "I can't sing," or "I'm just not musical," and withdraws completely. The adult feels defeated or incompetent. Often, they've internalised shame or repeated criticism, and now avoid trying at all.

These behaviours can feel frustrating, especially when we're trying to create a joyful, shared experience. But they aren't about the music. They're about the child's deeper needs.

> "I didn't realise how much my own embarrassment around singing was shaping my daughter's reluctance to join in. When I softened, she did too."

Music as a Mirror

Music often brings strong feelings to the surface — not only for children, but for us as adults. When a child's musical behaviour triggers us, it's worth pausing to ask: What might this be reflecting?

A child refusing to sing might remind us of a time we were shamed for our voice. A loud, repetitive tune might strike a nerve if we were told as children that noise was bad. Sometimes, we project our discomfort onto our children, labelling their expression as a problem when it's simply unfamiliar or unfiltered.

> "I always hushed my son when he sang at the table. Then I remembered: that was the only time I was allowed to sing growing

~ *Interlude* ~

In Practice: A Role Play of Recognition

In a workshop, we explored two versions of the same moment.

A parent stepped into the role of a seven-year-old child. They stood up and began to sing:

"La la la la la..."

In the **first version**, the 'adults' in the role play responded like this:

"Oh no, not again. You've sung that one already."
"Why can't you sing like your cousin? They're in the choir."
"Inside voices, please."

The group watching went still. One person whispered, *"That just hurt to watch."*

Then we tried again.

Same child. Same made-up melody.

"La la la la la..."

But this time, the 'adults' responded differently:

"Hey, that's a new one. I haven't heard that song before."
"Sing it again — I want to hear the ending."
"Sounds like your own song. Want to show me the dance that goes with it?"

The room softened. There was laughter. A few people welled up.

One person said quietly, *"I wish I'd had that."*

Part Three: Holding the Bigger Picture

Chapter 11

When the Song is Silenced

> *"He started rapping really loudly and aggressively. It was the only way he felt heard."*

Not every child sings freely. Not every parent feels able to sing. In many families, music has gone quiet — not by choice, but by circumstance. Trauma can silence the song.

Sometimes it's a single event. Sometimes it's the echo of generations. A parent who was shamed for singing off-key may still hear that inner critic. A child who's been yelled at for being "too loud" may learn to sing only in their head. The silence we meet is not always voluntary.

What Trauma Does

Trauma — whether acute, ongoing, or inherited — changes how the brain and body respond to the world. It shifts us into survival states: fight, flight, freeze, or fawn. In these states, creativity, play, and spontaneous expression often shut down.

Neurologically, the areas of the brain responsible for language, rhythm, and self-expression (such as Broca's area and the prefrontal cortex) may become less active under stress. The limbic system, especially the amygdala, becomes dominant — scanning for danger, not for harmony. Music, with its emotional intensity, can feel unsafe. Or it can be the very thing that brings us back.

"I didn't sing for years. Then one day, rocking my baby, the song just came out. It was mine, and it was hers. And I cried."

The Role of Safety

Recovery — from personal trauma or generational silencing — doesn't begin with performance. It begins with safety.

Safety in this context is not just physical. It's emotional and relational. It means creating space where the body can breathe, the voice can tremble, and there's no judgment.

Attuned, musical connection activates the vagus nerve, supports co-regulation, and restores access to parts of the brain linked with language and creativity (Porges, 2011; van der Kolk, 2014). Lullabies, rocking rhythms, humming, and drumming — all these have been used across cultures to soothe and heal.

> "Music was how my grandmother survived. She sang through war, through loss. Her lullaby came to me when I didn't know what else to do with my son's tears."

Being With What's Hard

Some children resist music because they've associated it with shame, ridicule, or overstimulation. Some parents feel grief when their child doesn't join in. Others feel rage when their child's expression brings up their own wounds.

It's okay.

This isn't a test to pass. It's a path to walk gently.

Start where you are. If all you can do is tap a rhythm together while waiting for the kettle to boil, that's enough. If you can hum while folding laundry, that counts. If you can sing a few notes in the dark, under your breath, you've begun.

> "When my child sang, I used to feel like I couldn't breathe. Now I know why. I was never allowed to make noise. I'm learning to breathe again."

Reflection Questions

- What memories or feelings surface for you when your child sings?
- Have there been times when music felt unsafe — for you or for them?
- What would a small step toward musical safety look like in your home?

Music doesn't require healing to be present. But it can be a companion in the healing. It waits patiently. It doesn't demand. It invites.

Even when it's gone quiet, the song is never lost. It's waiting — for breath, for welcome, for rhythm to return.

Chapter 12

When Words Aren't There

Music as Witness, Movement, and Meaning

"Music lets me feel things I didn't even know I was holding."

Music has an extraordinary ability to express and hear what we're feeling — even when we have no words. This isn't accidental. It's built into our bodies, in resonant frequencies and rhythmic patterns that help us feel, connect, and release.

In my twenties, I used to drive around with Alanis Morissette at full volume, screaming along to her lyrics. That music bore witness to my confusion, anger, and sadness. It let me scream in harmony with someone who felt like she understood.

Other days, it was Karen Carpenter. Her voice sang truths I hadn't found the words for yet. Even now, in low moments, I can put her music on in the kitchen and quietly weep to a grief I didn't realise I was still holding — and feel better afterwards.

That is part of the essential healing nature of music.

Music can do many things:

- It witnesses us. It offers company in feelings we cannot explain.
- It holds the emotions too big for our daily conversations.
- It moves what feels stuck. Emotion into motion.

For a hurting creative soul — child or adult — music can become a refuge, a way of working things out without being told what to feel or how to fix it.

Try This:

- Let your child repeat the same song if they're asking for it. It might be doing a job.
- Make space for your own music too — the songs that speak for you.
- Try listening together during tricky times. No need to talk — just be in it together.
- Notice what happens when you turn the music *off*. What feelings rise?

Something to consider

It's worth noticing when music helps us feel — and when we might be using it to avoid feeling. With recorded music available 24/7, it's tempting to keep the background noise going constantly. But there's a difference between *meeting* emotions and *masking* them.

Music that helps us feel is different from music that helps us avoid.

I catch myself sometimes and notice, what's needed is not another distraction — but a quiet moment, a shared song, or the stillness that lets emotion rise.

And sometimes, the music that helps most is the music we make together — live, acoustic, imperfect. Human.

This is how it has always been. Since the dawn of time, people have gathered around the fire, with drums, voices, sticks, claps.
 Not to perform. To be together.

Reflection Questions

- What music helps you feel, rather than escape?
- How do you know when a song is doing emotional work for you?
- What would it feel like to sit with your child and just *listen*?

Chapter 13

Sacred Sound, Silent Song

Music, Values, and Cultural Messages

> *"I was raised not to sing out loud, especially as a girl. I thought I was protecting my daughter. But she needed me to sing with her, not just keep her quiet."*

Not all families speak of music in the same way. For some, music is central to celebration, ritual, and everyday life. For others, it's treated with caution — as something worldly, distracting, or even forbidden. In many traditions, music is divided: sacred or profane, permitted or prohibited, male or female, public or private.

As parents, we carry those messages — even if we no longer consciously agree with them.

This chapter does not aim to define what's right. Instead, it offers space to reflect on the beliefs you inherited, the ones you're living now, and the ones you're growing into.

Messages We Receive

You may have heard, "Don't be noisy," or "Only professionals sing." Perhaps in your childhood home, music was something for men, or for special days, or only for prayer.
 Or maybe it was everywhere — but now you're unsure what's okay to pass on.

One parent from our workshop shared:

> "My daughter would sing all the time. I realised I was always telling her to stop. Not because it was wrong — just because it was unfamiliar to me. I didn't grow up in a singing home."

Another told a story of being hushed over and over until she stopped trying:

> "Even now, I whisper my own songs. It's like I'm not allowed to take up that kind of space."

Cultural Codes Around Music

Across cultures, we find deep and varied codes about music:

- In some Islamic communities, instrumental music is discouraged, while sung devotion (nasheeds, recitation) is deeply honoured.
- In Orthodox Jewish tradition, women may not sing in front of men after a certain age — yet lullabies and Sabbath songs are central in the home.
- In many Indigenous traditions, music is a sacred story. Some songs are not to be recorded or sung outside of specific settings.
- In Christian history, there have been periods when drums, dancing, and even harmony were treated as dangerous or profane — while other branches elevated full-body gospel worship.

These differences don't mean music is "good" or "bad." They remind us that music is powerful. And power is often regulated.

What Is Sacred in Your Home?

You may not have religious guidelines, but every family has values. Some homes revere silence. Some revere joy. Some treat ritual with care.

This chapter invites you to reflect:

- What songs are safe in your home?
- Who gets to sing, and when?
- What emotions are welcomed through music — and which are hidden?
- What did you learn, silently or overtly, about whose voice matters?

Rediscovering Permission

Reconnecting with music may feel awkward if you've been taught it's not "for you." But children need to know that music is not just allowed — it is human.
 It can live alongside your values. It can be a form of reverence, expression, or joy. It doesn't need to be loud, exposed, or staged.
 Sometimes it's just you, humming softly in the kitchen, and your child hearing: "I am safe. My parent is here."

Try This

Write down one musical memory from your childhood — joyful or painful. Then write one musical hope for your child. See if there's a gap between them. Does anything surprise you?

In Practice

If you're unsure about singing in front of others, start alone. Sing during routines. Use gentle sound without lyrics — humming or soft vowel sounds. You are not performing. You are grounding yourself and your child.

When we sing to a baby, we are saying: I see you. I'm here. We breathe together.

When we play with sound, we are saying: We are safe. We belong.

When we listen, we are saying: Your voice matters.

And when we repair — after rupture, after silence — we are saying: The music lives on.

This isn't sentimental. It's neurological. Polyvagal theory (Porges, 2011) shows us how music regulates the nervous system. Interpersonal neurobiology (Siegel, 2012) teaches us how rhythm and co-regulation shape the brain. Montessori, Kodály, and Dalcroze offer pedagogies that honour the child's whole sensory and emotional world. Music is not decoration. It is connection, restoration, and growth.

> "Even when I couldn't say what I needed, I could sing it."

What Now?

You don't need perfect pitch. You don't need to be "musical." You need presence. Curiosity. Courage.

Start where you are:

- Hum as you fold laundry.
- Clap a rhythm while you wait in line.
- Ask your child what their favourite sound is.
- Let them hear your voice, just as it is.

There is no wrong place to begin — only moments waiting to be reclaimed.

Questions

What did you discover about yourself through this journey?
- What part of the eternal song have you reclaimed?
- How might music continue to live in your family — quietly or joyfully, playfully or powerfully?

The eternal song is not something we give to children. It's something we remember together. Across generations. Across cultures. Across silence.

Let this be your invitation. Not to do more — but to return. To listen. To sing again. To be in rhythm with the child before you.

The song is already there.

Glossary of Gentle Definiti

Attunement
The process of being deeply in sync with your child — noticing moods, rhythms, and signals, and responding with care. Like a tuning fork, you vibrate together.

Co-regulation
When a calm adult helps a child manage their big feelings by offering steady presence, touch, or voice. We regulate together, not alone.

Embodied
Lived and felt in the body. Embodied music means the rhythm is not just heard — it's swayed to, rocked with, breathed in.

Holding Space
Being fully present with someone's emotions or experience without trying to fix, distract, or judge. A quiet kind of support.

Interpersonal Neurobiology
A science of how relationships shape the brain. Our interactions — especially early ones — help wire a child's sense of safety and connection.

Lullaby
A gentle, soothing song. Often sung to babies, but just as meaningful for toddlers, teens, and tired grown-ups. It's less about the tune, more about the comfort.

Mistaken Goal (Adlerian)
A term from parenting psychology. When children seek attention, power, revenge or withdrawal, they may be expressing an unmet need — not being "naughty."

Musicality
Your natural ability to respond to rhythm, melody, and tone. Every human has this — it's not about being a "musician."

Self-regulation
A child's developing ability to manage their emotions, energy and attention. First learned through co-regulation with loving adults.

Trauma-informed
An approach that recognises how past stress or harm can affect behaviour. It replaces judgment with curiosity and care.

Continue Exploring

These are offered not as homework, but as doorways. Go where your curiosity leads…

Discography & Listening List

A collection of named songs and artists mentioned throughout the book and in our workshops, drawn from personal stories, examples, and suggested listening.

Songs from the Text

- "Zombie" – The Cranberries
- "Hello" – Fayrouz (Arabic version, emotional resonance)
- "Affirmation" – Savage Garden
- "We Could Have Been Anything That We Wanted to Be" – *Bugsy Malone* soundtrack

References and Further Reading

Adler, A. (1998). *Understanding Human Nature*. Oneworld Publications.

Nelsen, J (2006). *Positive Discipline: The Classic Guide to Helping Children Develop Self-Discipline, Responsibility, Cooperation, and Problem-Solving Skills.* Random House Publishing Group

Bailey, B. (2000). *Conscious Discipline: 7 Basic Skills for Brain Smart Classroom Management*. Loving Guidance.

Bergese, A., & Darvas, F. (2016). *Rhythm, Music and the Brain: Scientific Foundations and Clinical Applications*. Springer.

Bruscia, K. E. (1998). *Defining Music Therapy*. Barcelona Publishers.

Cozolino, L. (2014). *The Neuroscience of Human Relationships*. Norton.

Dalcroze, E. J. (1921). *Rhythm, Music and Education*. G. P. Putnam's Sons.

Delahooke, Mona (2020). *Beyond Behaviors: Using Brain Science and Compassion to Understand and Solve Children's Behavioural Challenges* Sheldon Press.

Elkind, D. (2007). *The Power of Play*. Da Capo Lifelong Books.

Gabor, M., & Mate, D. (2022). *The Myth of Normal: Trauma, Illness & Healing in a Toxic Culture*. Vermilion.

Goddard-Blyth, S. (2018) *Movement: Your Child's First Language: How music and movement assist brain development in children aged 3-7 years (Hawthorn Press Early Years).* Hawthorn Press.

Greenspan, S. I., & Benderly, B. L. (1997). *The Growth of the Mind and the Endangered Origins of Intelligence*. Perseus.

Kabat-Zinn, J. (1994). *Wherever You Go, There You Are*. Hyperion.

Kirkland, K., & Mitchell, C. (2015). *Montessori and Early Childhood: A*

Guide for Students. SAGE Publications.

Koelsch, S. (2012). *Brain and Music*. Wiley.

Kuhn, D. (2002). *The Music of the Brain: The Role of Music in the Development of the Infant Brain*. Early Childhood Connections, 8(1).

Levitin, D. (2019). *This is Your Brain on Music: Understanding a Human Obsession*. Penguin

Montessori, M. (1967). *The Absorbent Mind*. Holt Paperbacks.

Panksepp, J. (2009). *Affective Neuroscience: The Foundations of Human and Animal Emotions*. Oxford University Press.

Partanen, E., Kujala, T., Tervaniemi, M., & Huotilainen, M. (2013). Prenatal music exposure induces long-term neural effects. *PLoS ONE, 8*(10).

Perry, B. D., & Szalavitz, M. (2006). *The Boy Who Was Raised as a Dog*. Basic Books.

Porges, S. W. (2011). *The Polyvagal Theory: Neurophysiological Foundations of Emotions, Attachment, Communication, Self-regulation*. Norton.

Siegel, D. J. (2012). *The Developing Mind: How Relationships and the Brain Interact to Shape Who We Are*. Guilford Press.

Stern, D. N. (2004). *The Present Moment in Psychotherapy and Everyday Life*. Norton.

Trevarthen, C. (1999). Musicality and the intrinsic motive pulse: Evidence from human psychobiology and infant communication. *Musicae Scientiae, 3*(1), 155–215.

van der Kolk, B. (2014). *The Body Keeps the Score: Brain, Mind, and Body in the Healing of Trauma*. Viking.

Zentner, M., & Eerola, T. (2010). Rhythmic engagement with music in infancy. *Proceedings of the National Academy of Sciences, 107*(13), 5768–5773.

Stay Connected

If you've found something meaningful in these pages, I'd love to hear from you. Your reflections help this work keep growing.

- Visit: www.gcpdtrainer.co.uk

- Share this book with someone else who might need a reminder that music lives in us all.

Thank you for walking this path through song, silence, story and sound. Whether you've sung along, reflected quietly, or simply carried these ideas in your mind as you moved through your days — you've already begun.

There is no perfect way to bring music into family life. It's not about hitting the right notes, but about tuning in — to yourself, your child, and the moment you're in together. Trust that what you bring is enough. You are already part of the song.

About the Author

Gillian Corke is a Trainer for the Positive Discipline Association, a Montessori assistant and Creative Directress with over a decade of experience in Montessori environments, and a lifelong musician. She is an educator, and creative facilitator working at the intersection of sound, movement, and relational learning. Gillian has taught swimming, designed and delivered international personal-development programmes for Torke Cycling, and supported children one-to-one through INPP reflex-integration. A musician and educator for nearly 30 years, Gillian specializes in Dalcroze- and Kodály-informed music-movement integration and trauma-informed parent–child therapy. Author of *Out of the Box: Music, Movement and Meaning in the Montessori Classroom* and *Supporting Your Children in Sport*, she brings neuroscience, experiential learning, and creative facilitation to empower children and educators alike.

Also by the Author

Out of the Box: Music, Movement, and Meaning in the Montessori Classroom

A practical and thoughtful resource for educators and caregivers exploring music and movement within early childhood environments, grounded in Montessori philosophy and enriched by embodied practice.

Moving Minds: Integrating Physical Activity into Montessori Elementary

Blending classic Montessori principles with cutting-edge neurobiology and real-world stories from classrooms, forests, and sports fields, this book offers a transformative approach to whole-child development.

Printed in Dunstable, United Kingdom